The Little Net Book

By Cathy Coulter

Web Site	
ID:	Password:

Web Site	
ID:	Password:

Web Site	
ID:	Password:

Web Site	
ID:	Password:

Web Site	
ID:	Password:

Web Site	
ID:	Password:

Web Site	
ID:	Password:

Web Site	
ID:	Password:
Web Site	
ID:	Password:
Web Site	
ID:	Password:
Web Site	
ID:	Password:
Web Site	
ID:	Password:
Web Site	
ID:	Password:
Web Site	
ID:	Password:

Web Site	
ID:	Password:

Web Site	
ID:	Password:

Web Site	
ID:	Password:

Web Site	
ID:	Password:

Web Site	
ID:	Password:

Web Site	
ID:	Password:

Web Site	
ID:	Password:

Web Site	
ID:	Password:

Web Site	
ID:	Password:

Web Site	
ID:	Password:

Web Site	
ID:	Password:

Web Site	
ID:	Password:

Web Site	
ID:	Password:

Web Site	
ID:	Password:

Web Site	
ID:	Password:

Web Site	
ID:	Password:

Web Site	
ID:	Password:

Web Site	
ID:	Password:

Web Site	
ID:	Password:

Web Site	
ID:	Password:

Web Site	
ID:	Password:

Web Site	
ID:	Password:

Web Site	
ID:	Password:

Web Site	
ID:	Password:

Web Site	
ID:	Password:

Web Site	
ID:	Password:

Web Site	
ID:	Password:

Web Site	
ID:	Password:

Web Site	
ID:	Password:

Web Site	
ID:	Password:

Web Site	
ID:	Password:

Web Site	
ID:	Password:

Web Site	
ID:	Password:

Web Site	
ID:	Password:

Web Site	
ID:	Password:

Web Site			
ID:		Password:	
Web Site			
ID:		Password:	
Web Site			
ID:		Password:	
Web Site			
ID:		Password:	
Web Site			
ID:		Password:	
Web Site			
ID:		Password:	
Web Site			
ID:		Password:	

Web Site	
ID:	Password:

Web Site	
ID:	Password:

Web Site	
ID:	Password:

Web Site	
ID:	Password:

Web Site	
ID:	Password:

Web Site	
ID:	Password:

Web Site	
ID:	Password:

Web Site	
ID:	Password:

Web Site	
ID:	Password:

Web Site	
ID:	Password:

Web Site	
ID:	Password:

Web Site	
ID:	Password:

Web Site	
ID:	Password:

Web Site	
ID:	Password:

Web Site	
ID:	Password:

Web Site	
ID:	Password:

Web Site	
ID:	Password:

Web Site	
ID:	Password:

Web Site	
ID:	Password:

Web Site	
ID:	Password:

Web Site	
ID:	Password:

Web Site			
ID:		Password:	
Web Site			
ID:		Password:	
Web Site			
ID:		Password:	
Web Site			
ID:		Password:	
Web Site			
ID:		Password:	
Web Site			
ID:		Password:	
Web Site			
ID:		Password:	

Web Site	
ID:	Password:

Web Site	
ID:	Password:

Web Site	
ID:	Password:

Web Site	
ID:	Password:

Web Site	
ID:	Password:

Web Site	
ID:	Password:

Web Site	
ID:	Password:

Web Site	
ID:	Password:

Web Site	
ID:	Password:

Web Site	
ID:	Password:

Web Site	
ID:	Password:

Web Site	
ID:	Password:

Web Site	
ID:	Password:

Web Site	
ID:	Password:

Web Site	
ID:	Password:

Web Site	
ID:	Password:

Web Site	
ID:	Password:

Web Site	
ID:	Password:

Web Site	
ID:	Password:

Web Site	
ID:	Password:

Web Site	
ID:	Password:

Web Site	
ID:	Password:

Web Site	
ID:	Password:

Web Site	
ID:	Password:

Web Site	
ID:	Password:

Web Site	
ID:	Password:

Web Site	
ID:	Password:

Web Site	
ID:	Password:

Web Site	
ID:	Password:

Web Site	
ID:	Password:

Web Site	
ID:	Password:

Web Site	
ID:	Password:

Web Site	
ID:	Password:

Web Site	
ID:	Password:

Web Site	
ID:	Password:

Web Site			
ID:		Password:	
Web Site			
ID:		Password:	
Web Site			
ID:		Password:	
Web Site			
ID:		Password:	
Web Site			
ID:		Password:	
Web Site			
ID:		Password:	
Web Site			
ID:		Password:	

Web Site	
ID:	Password:
Web Site	
ID:	Password:
Web Site	
ID:	Password:
Web Site	
ID:	Password:
Web Site	
ID:	Password:
Web Site	
ID:	Password:
Web Site	
ID:	Password:

Web Site	
ID:	Password:

Web Site	
ID:	Password:

Web Site	
ID:	Password:

Web Site	
ID:	Password:

Web Site	
ID:	Password:

Web Site	
ID:	Password:

Web Site	
ID:	Password:

Web Site	
ID:	Password:

Web Site	
ID:	Password:

Web Site	
ID:	Password:

Web Site	
ID:	Password:

Web Site	
ID:	Password:

Web Site	
ID:	Password:

Web Site	
ID:	Password:

Web Site	
ID:	Password:
Web Site	
ID:	Password:
Web Site	
ID:	Password:
Web Site	
ID:	Password:
Web Site	
ID:	Password:
Web Site	
ID:	Password:
Web Site	
ID:	Password:

Web Site			
ID:		Password:	
Web Site			
ID:		Password:	
Web Site			
ID:		Password:	
Web Site			
ID:		Password:	
Web Site			
ID:		Password:	
Web Site			
ID:		Password:	
Web Site			
ID:		Password:	

Web Site	
ID:	Password:

Web Site	
ID:	Password:

Web Site	
ID:	Password:

Web Site	
ID:	Password:

Web Site	
ID:	Password:

Web Site	
ID:	Password:

Web Site	
ID:	Password:

www.ingramcontent.com/pod-product-compliance
Lightning Source LLC
Chambersburg PA
CBHW071346310526
45790CB00018B/1376